Little

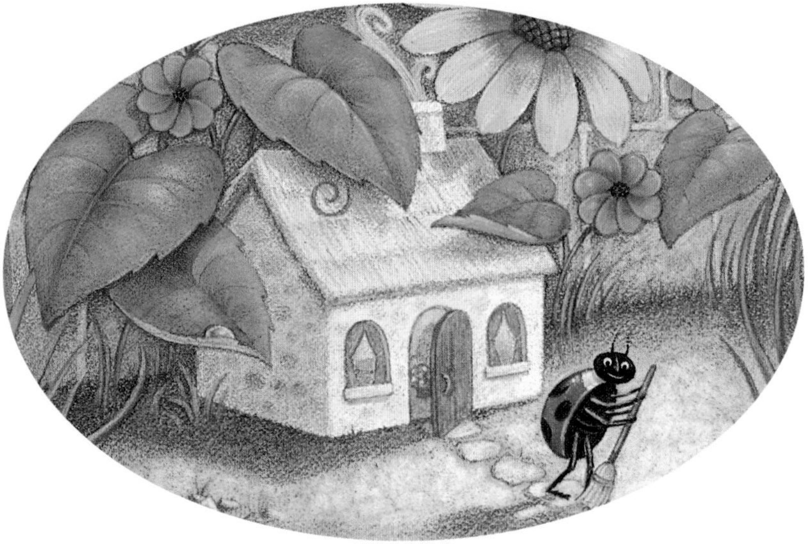

Written by **Polly Peterson** • Illustrated by **Kathi Ember**

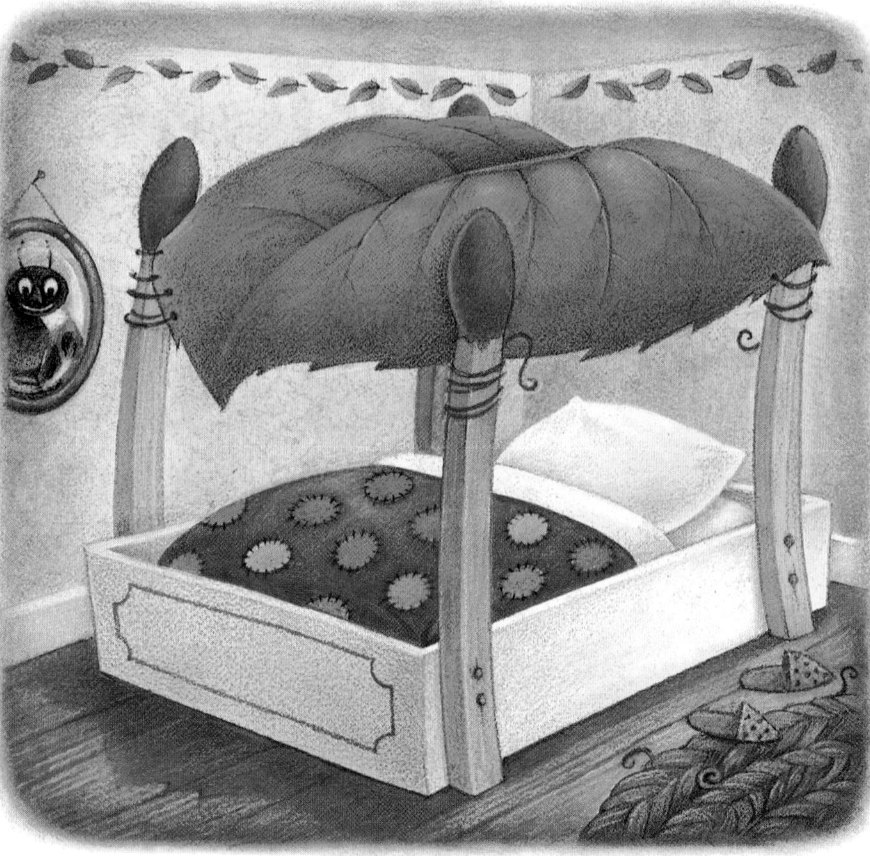

Little bed,

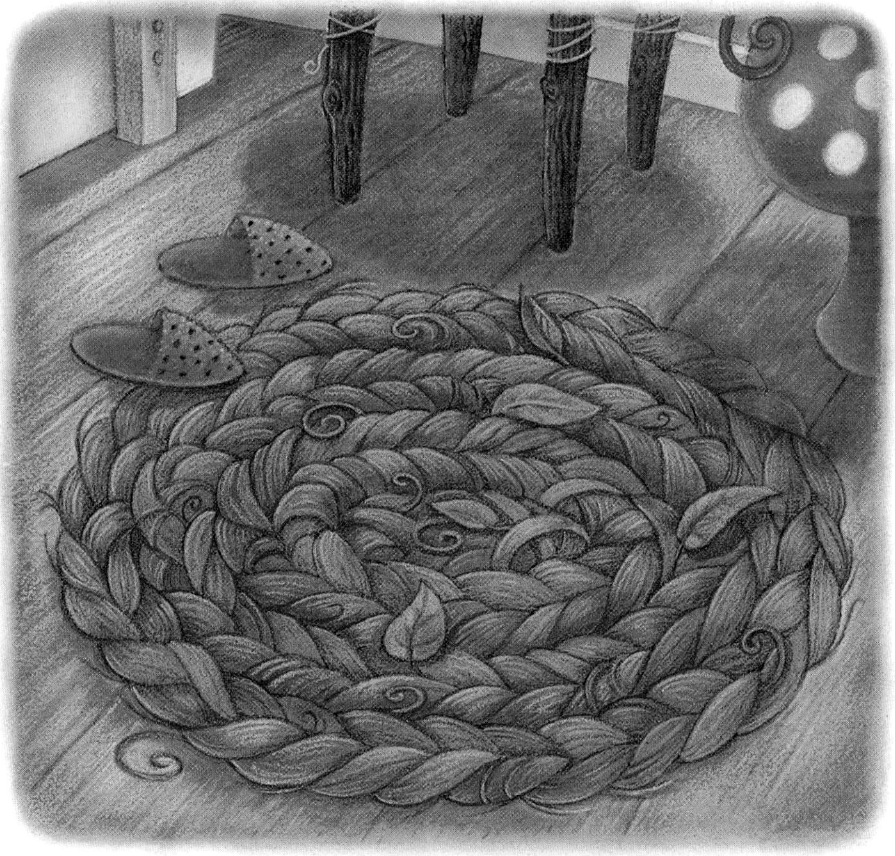

little rug,

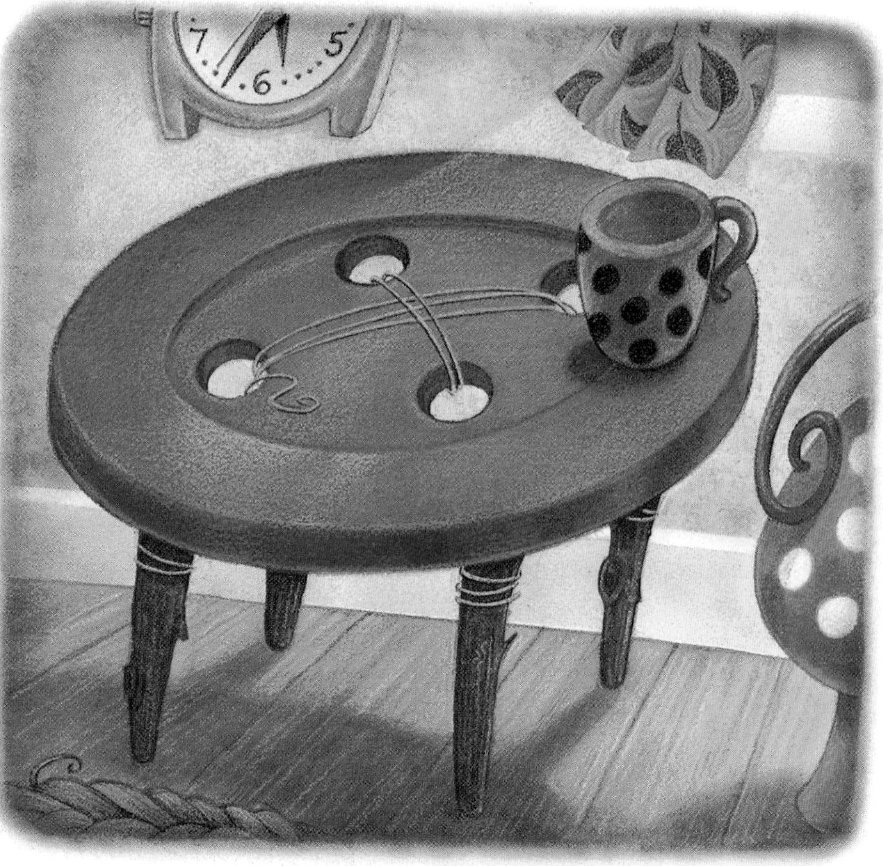

little table,

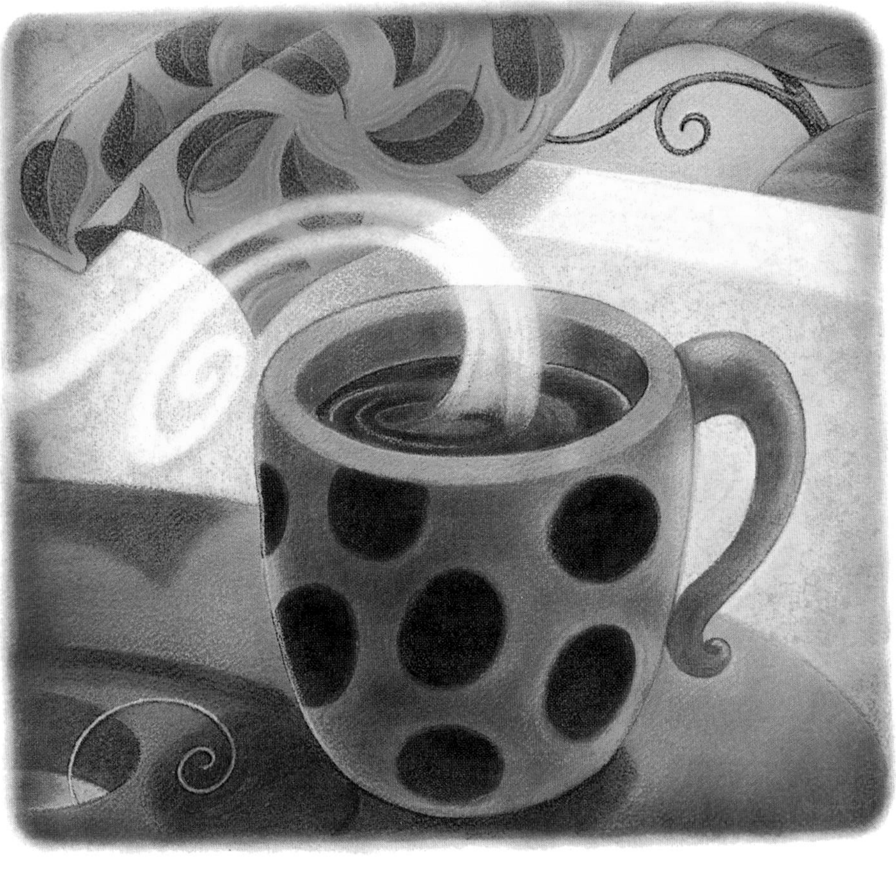

little mug,

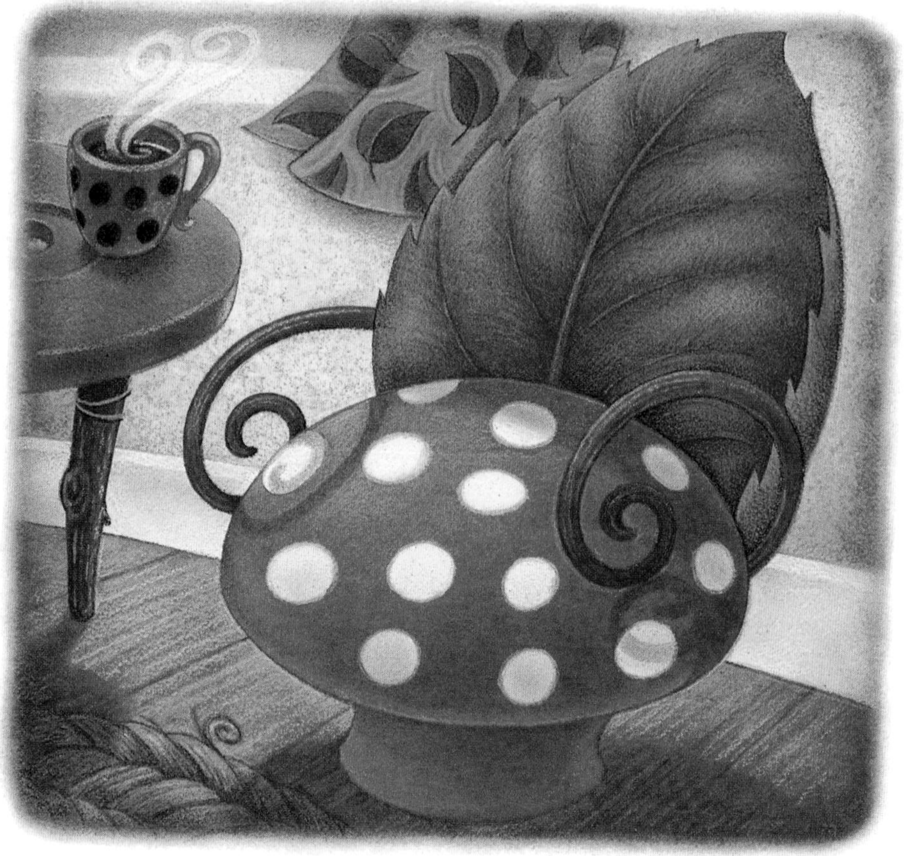

little chair,

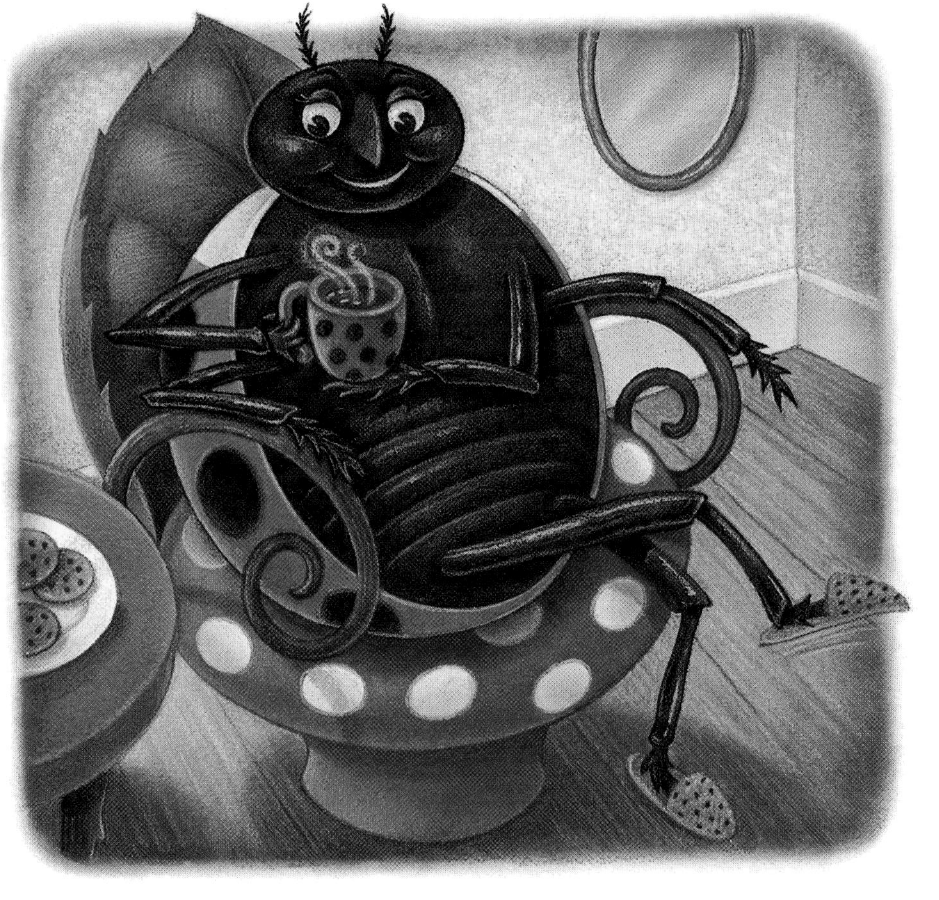

little bug,

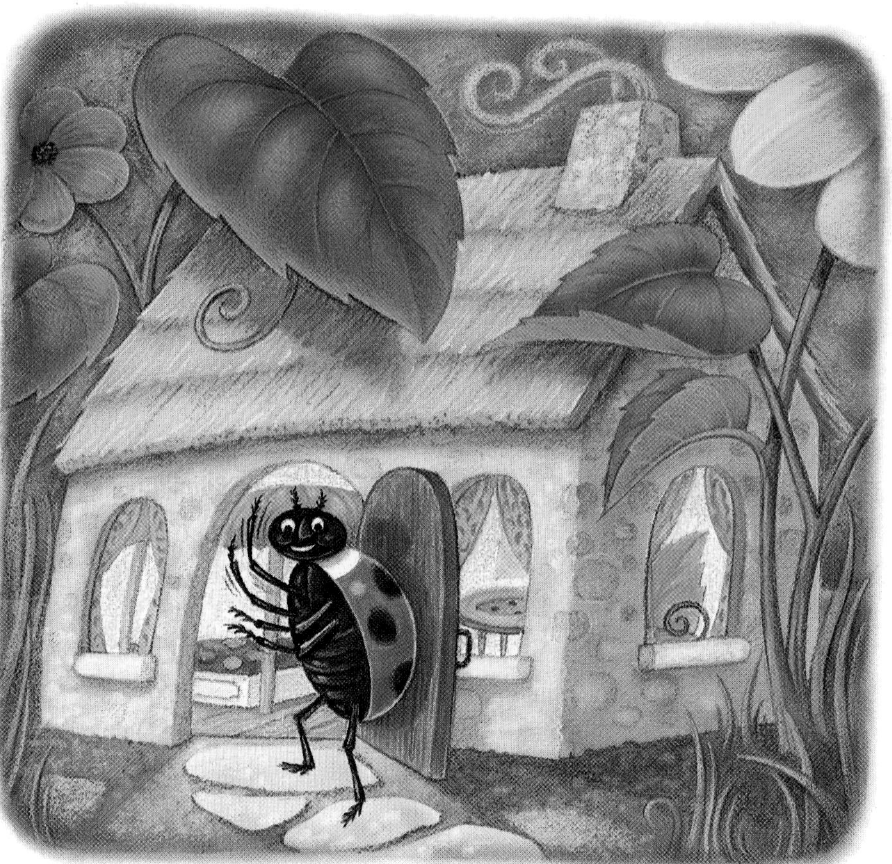

little house.